UNEARTHING ANCIENT CIVILIZATIONS

ANCIENT INDIA REVEALED

BY DONNA REYNOLDS

Cavendish Square
New York

Published in 2023 by Cavendish Square Publishing, LLC
29 E. 21st Street, New York, NY 10010

First Edition

Website: cavendishsq.com

Library of Congress Cataloging-in-Publication Data

Names: Reynolds, Donna, author.
Title: Ancient India revealed / by Donna Reynolds.
Description: New York : Cavendish Square Publishing, [2023]. | Series: Unearthing ancient civilizations | Includes index.
Identifiers: LCCN 2021052122 | ISBN 9781502666147 (library binding) | ISBN 9781502666123 (paperback) | ISBN 9781502666130 (set) | ISBN 9781502666154 (ebook)
Subjects: LCSH: India–History–Juvenile literature. | India–Civilization–Juvenile literature.
Classification: LCC DS436 .R49 2023 | DDC 934–dc23/eng/20211026
LC record available at https://lccn.loc.gov/2021052122

Editor: Jennifer Lombardo
Copyeditor: Abby Young
Designer: Deanna Paternostro

The photographs in this book are used by permission and through the courtesy of: Cover, back cover effective stock photos/Shutterstock.com; p. 4 gt29/Shutterstock.com; p. 6 suronin/Shutterstock.com; pp. 8-9 Daksh Pandya Exhibit/Shutterstock.com; p. 10 User-duck/Wikimedia Commons; p. 12 saiko3p/Shutterstock.com; pp. 12–13 Michal Knitl/Shutterstock.com; p. 15 Gwoeii/Shutterstock.com; p. 16 Bhaven Jani/Shutterstock.com; p. 19 Alpha Travel Tales/Shutterstock.com; pp. 20–21 PetraKub/Shutterstock.com; p. 22 Carlos Amarillo/Shutterstock.com; p. 24 RudiErnst/Shutterstock.com; pp. 26–27 thirawatana phaisalratana/Shutterstock.com; p. 28 (top left) AlexelA/Shutterstock.com; p. 28 (bottom) explorewithinfo/Shutterstock.com; p. 28 (top right) NV Studio/Shutterstock.com.

CPSIA compliance information: Batch #CSCSQ23: For further information, contact Cavendish Square Publishing LLC, New York, New York, at 1-877-980-4450.

Printed in the United States of America

CONTENTS

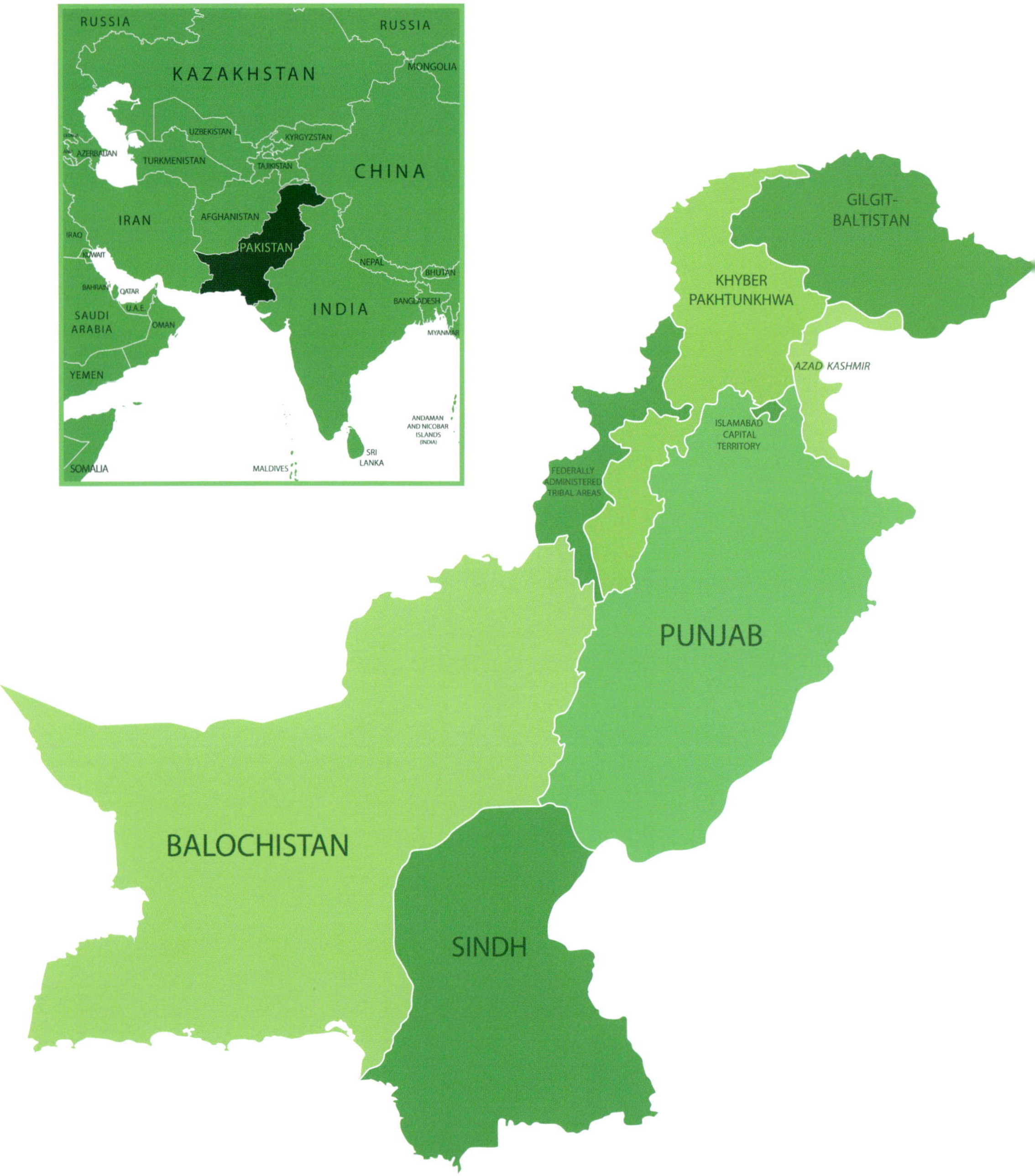

The country of Pakistan used to be part of India. Ancient India's two biggest cities were in what are now the Punjab and Sindh areas of Pakistan.

CHAPTER ONE
THE FIRST CIVILIZATION

Like many ancient civilizations, ancient India was created near a river. India's main river is called the Indus, which is how the country got its name. It is one of the three major rivers of the Indian **subcontinent**. People have lived in the areas that are now India and Pakistan since about 60,000 BCE, but it was not until about 7000 BCE that these small settlements first began to turn into a larger civilization.

FARMS AND CITIES

Experts have divided ancient Indian history into several periods. Between about 7000 and 5500 BCE, people began to farm along the Indus River. They built villages and raised goats, sheep, and cattle. This time period is called the pre-Harappan period. By about 5500 BCE, these villagers had started trading with neighboring areas, and the civilization entered what is now called the Early Harappan period. The name comes from the city of Harappa, which was built around 2800 BCE. It was the first ancient Indian city **archaeologists** found in modern times. This civilization is also often called the Indus valley civilization because of its location.

The cities the ancient Indians built were very advanced for their time. They had well-planned streets, indoor bathrooms, and sewer systems that ran throughout the city. The Indus valley cities all look very similar, and their parts are **standardized**, which shows that a group—possibly a central government—planned them out carefully. For example, roads and bricks are all the same size, and the streets are laid out in a grid that is easy to follow. Harappa and another city called Mohenjo-daro may have had as many as 50,000 people living in them. This is a huge population for that time! Most ancient cities had a population of about 10,000.

Ancient Indian cities such as Mohenjo-daro (*shown here*) were very carefully and neatly built.

A HISTORY MYSTERY

Archaeologists have found items with writing on them where the Harappan civilization used to be. They called the writing Indus script. However, no one has ever been able to decipher, or learn how to read, Indus script. Experts who have spent years trying to decipher it have guesses about what the written records say, but they may never know for sure. This is a major reason why we know so much more about other ancient civilizations, including Egypt, China, Mesopotamia, and Rome.

MAKING GUESSES

Not much is known about the people who were part of the Indus valley civilization. One reason for this is that no one can read their writing. Another is that archaeologists uncovered it much later than they did with other ancient civilizations. For a long time, people believed there were no civilizations in ancient India. By the time Harappa was uncovered in 1829 CE, experts had already uncovered ancient Egypt and Mesopotamia.

As they started looking into Harappa, however, they soon realized that it was even older and more advanced than the civilizations that had been found first. Many people now think that the things we believe were first done by the Egyptians and Mesopotamians were actually first done by the Indians.

THE FALL OF THE INDUS VALLEY

Another thing experts are unsure of is why the Indus valley civilization started to **decline** around 1900 BCE. By about 1700 BCE, the people had abandoned many of their cities. For many years, experts thought a group called the Aryans attacked.

For thousands of years, the remains of buildings of the Indus valley civilization, such as this one, were hidden.

However, new information showed that the Aryans most likely came to the area peacefully. Today, experts think the civilization

declined and fell because of one or more of the following reasons: climate change, overcrowded cities, or a decline in trade with Egypt and Mesopotamia. As they continue to study Harappa and other ancient Indus valley cities, they will learn more.

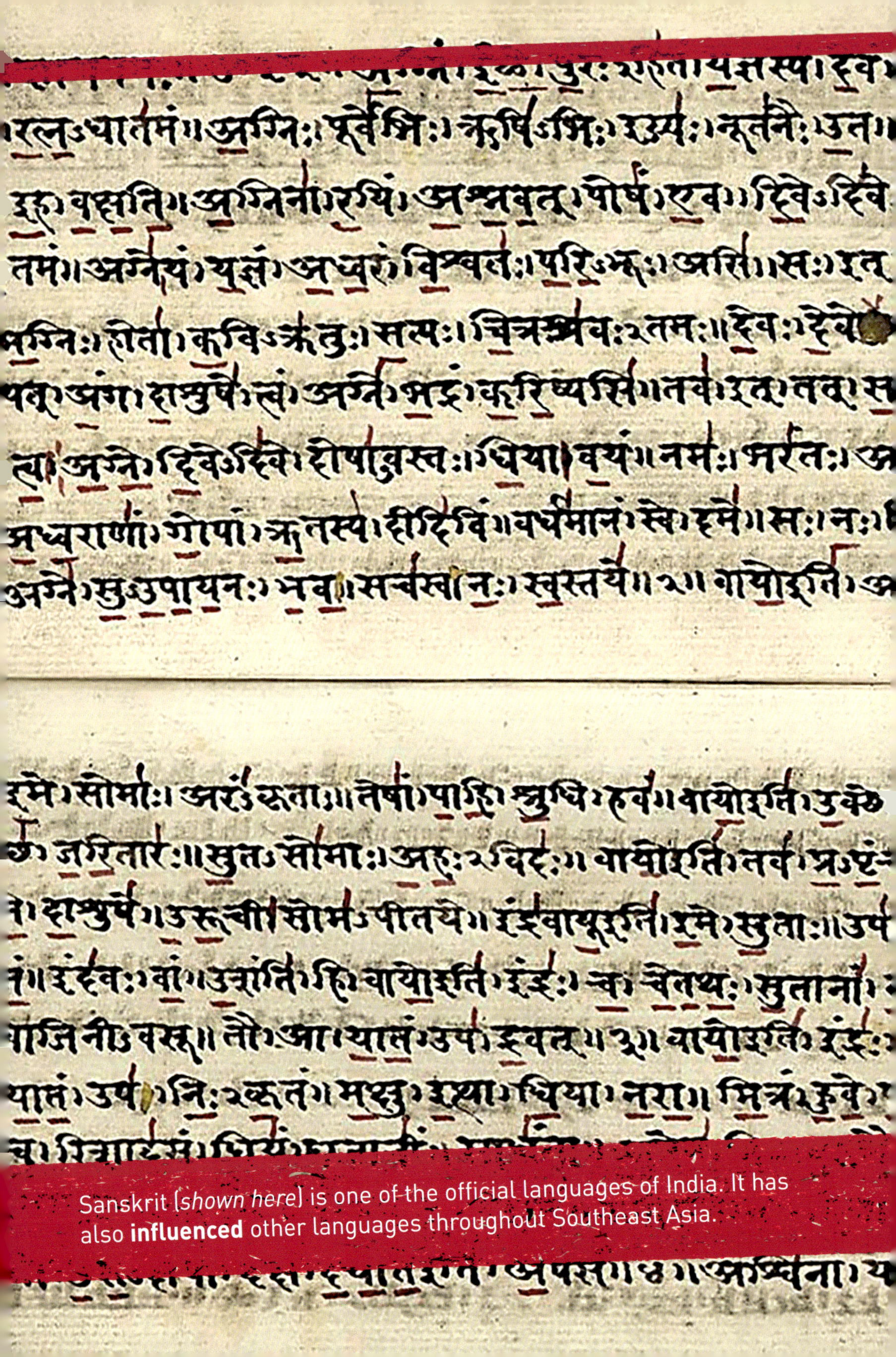

Sanskrit (*shown here*) is one of the official languages of India. It has also **influenced** other languages throughout Southeast Asia.

CHAPTER TWO

THE VEDIC CIVILIZATION

After the Indus valley civilization fell, the Aryans created a new civilization that is now called the Vedic civilization. "Vedic" comes from the Vedas, which were the books of beliefs the people followed. Like the Christian Bible, the Vedas also recorded some things that happened in history. Because experts know how to read the writing used in the Vedas, which is called Sanskrit, we know a little more about them than about the Indus valley people. However, many historians and archaeologists still disagree about certain things.

A DIFFERENT WAY OF LIFE

Most experts believe the Aryans came from what is now the country of Iran. This is because there are some similarities between the languages and religions, or belief systems, of the two civilizations.

The Indus valley people had lived in large cities, and they traded things they made with people from other areas. The Aryans lived in small villages, and they mainly raised cattle. In fact, the early Vedic people believed cows were a **symbol** of the gods. Cows are still considered sacred, or holy, to many Indians today.

The main way experts know about the Indus valley civilization is through archaeology. However, the main way they know about the Vedic civilization is through their writings. The early Vedas tell us that the Aryans had a leader who was called a king but was elected by the people. Only nobles could be elected king. The king's main jobs were to protect his people, collect their taxes, and decide what the taxes would be used for.

AN ANCIENT RELIGION

The Vedas tell us about Indian history, but they are mainly religious writings. Vedic gods and goddesses were said to control things such as social class, the sun, the wind, and the earth. Some Vedic beliefs are similar to the beliefs of an ancient Mesopotamian

Hindus have been coming to the Meenakshi Temple (*shown here*) for thousands of years to worship their gods. Every 12 years, the statues on the outside are cleaned and repainted to keep the temple looking like new.

religion called Zoroastrianism, which supports the idea that the Aryans came from Iran. A major part of the Vedic belief system was that the gods needed animal sacrifices to keep them happy. When they were unhappy, the gods would cause problems.

OLD RELIGION, NEW NAME

The beliefs the Vedic people followed were the beginning of the religion we know today as Hinduism. It is unclear how long people have been following this belief system, since there is no way to know if people of the Indus valley civilization practiced it. If they did, that would make Hinduism the oldest living religion in the world. However, the word "Hinduism" is very new. It was invented in the early 19th century by Europeans.

CREATING CASTES

One of the things the Vedas describe is very **strict** castes, or social classes. For thousands of years, the caste a person was born into told them where they could live, whom they could marry, what jobs they could do, and more. Today, the caste system is less strict, but many people still know what caste they are part of.

The Vedas described four castes. At the top, with the most wealth and power, were the Brahmins, who were priests and teachers. Under them were Kshatriyas, who were warriors and rulers. Third in line were Vaishyas, who were farmers and merchants. At the bottom were the Shudras, who did most of the hard labor. People who had no caste were called Dalits, or untouchables. The only jobs they were allowed to do were the ones no one else wanted, such as cleaning the streets and the toilets.

The word "Brahmin" comes from Hinduism's main god, Brahma (*shown here*).

Ancient Hindus believed this caste system came from the gods and was the only way to keep order in society. They believed that the caste a person was born into was determined by their actions in their past lives. If a person lived a good life as a Vaishya, they might come back in the next life as a Brahmin. If they lived a bad life, they might come back as a Dalit. Everyone was taught that this was a fair way for the world to work, so for years, many people accepted the caste system and did not try to change it.

The Ganges River (*shown here*) is still an important part of life in India.

CHAPTER THREE

KINGDOMS AND EMPIRES

Around 600 BCE, 16 kingdoms called Mahajanapadas began to rise in the Ganges River valley. They started as small tribes, or *janas*, that each decided to take control of specific parts of India. The areas that belonged to the janas were called *janapadas*. As they grew larger and took over some of the land around them, they became known as "great states," or Mahajanapadas.

THE 16 KINGDOMS

Although they are all called kingdoms, some of the 16 Mahajanapadas were democratic, meaning people who lived there could vote on the laws. The wealthiest and most powerful kingdom was called Magadha. This is where the religious leader known as Buddha spent much of his life, so the area is still very special to Buddhists. One of the reasons experts know about the Mahajanapadas is because they rose to power before Buddhism started, so they were written about in Buddhist religious writings.

ATTACKS FROM OUTSIDERS

Around 550 BCE, Cyrus the Great of Persia attacked and **conquered** the northwest part of India. Later rulers added a bit more of the country to their empire. This opened up trade between India and Persia, and Persian **culture** influenced Indian culture. However, when the Persians went to war with the Greeks, they had to stop moving further into India. Instead, they used Indians as soldiers to help fight against the Greeks.

India was attacked again in 327 BCE by Alexander the Great. By this time, Alexander had conquered Persia and added it to his own empire. When northwest India became part of this empire, the Mahajanapadas still existed, but they had lost most of their power.

A GOVERNMENT HANDBOOK

Chandragupta's main adviser was a man named Kautilya. He wrote a book called the *Arthashastra* to explain what he thought were the best ways for a government to stay in power. One thing the book mentioned was the importance of spies. Kautilya thought it was important for a king to have a lot of spies living with the people of his country so they could tell the king if anyone was not behaving well.

THE MAURYAN EMPIRE

Alexander the Great died in 323 BCE. Two years later, the Mauryan Empire rose to power. It was the first empire to cover most of the Indian subcontinent. It was named

The Barabar Caves (*shown here*) are believed to be the oldest man-made caves in the world. They were carved out of this rock during the Mauryan Empire.

after the person who started it: Chandragupta Maurya. Chandragupta conquered Magadha, took power, and started attacking the surrounding parts of India to add to his empire. Sometimes instead of attacking, he would form an alliance, or agreement, with the leader of the area he was trying to conquer.

THE GUPTA EMPIRE

Chandragupta's family ruled the Mauryan Empire until about 232 BCE. After the last leader died, the empire fell apart into many small kingdoms that often fought among

themselves. It was not until about 240 CE that another empire—the Gupta Empire—rose to power.

The rise of the Gupta Empire brought the Indian subcontinent peace and wealth. Its rulers spent money on the arts, math, and medicine. This created a golden age in ancient India. Visitors from outside India were often amazed by this wealthy, advanced empire. However, around 550 CE, a group called the White Huns attacked India. The Gupta Empire fell, and India again split into small kingdoms and was not brought together again until the 16th century.

The Udayagiri Caves (*shown here*) are the only place that experts can say for sure was built for a leader of the Gupta Empire.The caves hold some of the oldest Hindu temples and symbols in India.

This wooden carving shows Buddha sitting under the tree where he realized the Four Noble Truths.

CHAPTER FOUR

LASTING INVENTIONS

The ancient Indians created many things that are still around today. Some of these are **physical** things, but many are ideas or beliefs. These include games, math and science, ideas about the nature of life, the religion of Hinduism, and much more. Today, the things and ideas invented in ancient India have spread all over the world.

BUDDHISM

Like Hinduism, Buddhism began in India and spread throughout the world. Some people say Buddhism is a religion because it talks about behavior that can influence a person's afterlife. Others say it is only a way of life because Buddhists do not worship a god. Not everyone agrees on this point, but everyone can agree that Buddhism is based on the teachings of a man named Siddhartha Gautama. Gautama was a prince from a kingdom in northeast India. He became the first Buddha, or "**enlightened** one."

The main things Buddha taught are called the Four Noble Truths. These truths say that all life includes suffering; that this suffering is caused by being too attached to physical things and wanting them too much; that the end of suffering is called nirvana;

Buddhism does not have priests. The people who commit their lives to Buddhism are called monks. Children as young as six can become monks.

and that the way to reach nirvana is to do the right things. Buddha also told his followers to question everything they were told, even if he was the one who told it to them. He wanted them to find the truth for themselves, not just listen to what other people told them. Over the years, Buddhism spread throughout Asia and influenced the beliefs and ways of life of people in countries such as China, Japan, and Korea.

MATH AND SCIENCE

One of the things the ancient Indians invented that everyone in the world uses today is the number zero. In ancient India, the zero was used as a symbol for a Buddhist idea called *shunya*, which means "emptiness." Experts say other societies used a zero as a placeholder in numbers, but unlike the Indians, they did not use it to solve math problems and probably did not think it had any special meaning. Because the Indian zero came from the idea of emptiness, people today think of a zero as the symbol of having nothing.

HAVING FUN

Like everyone else in the world, the ancient Indians liked to have fun. Chess came from ancient India and is one of the oldest games we know of in the history of the world. The board games Ludo and Parcheesi both came from a game called pachisi, and a form of Chutes and Ladders also came from India. The ancient Indians also liked more physical games, such as badminton and polo. Ancient Indian rulers used to play polo on elephants, but today, the game is played on horses.

Ancient Indians were also some of the first in the world to study the stars. This science is called astronomy. Long before Europeans came up with the idea that the sun moves around Earth, some Indian astronomers suggested that it was the other way around, which is correct!

LANGUAGE AND ART

Because many people today can read Sanskrit, we know that the ancient Indians wrote about math and astronomy. They also wrote two epics in Sanskrit. An epic is a long poem that tells the story of a hero or the history of a country. India's epics are called the *Ramayana* and the *Mahabharata*. Experts believe they are partly based on real historical events. These two epics influenced the Hindu religion, and they are still famous today.

Another lasting Indian invention is a blue dye called indigo. The Greeks called this blue color *indikon*, which means "from India." The plant it comes from can only grow in warm places, so it was very valuable to merchants from Europe and other cold places. However, making indigo

Indigo dye was created by the ancient Indians. For thousands of years, no one else could make this beautiful deep blue.

dye was a long, difficult, and expensive process. This made indigo cloth so expensive that only the very wealthy could afford it, just like things that were dyed purple. Today, everyone can have a piece of indigo clothing! We know it as the color of most jeans.

HISTORY HAPPENED HERE

MOHENJO-DARO

- Mohenjo-daro is in Sindh, Pakistan.
- Harappa was discovered first, but Mohenjo-daro was one of the biggest Indus valley cities.
- The city was one of the most advanced in the Indus valley civilization.

MEENAKSHI TEMPLE

- The temple was first built in the 6th century BCE. It was rebuilt in the 16th century CE after it was destroyed by attackers.
- There are at least 33,000 statues on the temple.
- It is still used for worship in India today. Every year, 1 million people visit the temple during its festival in April. The rest of the year, the temple gets about 15,000 visitors most days.

NALANDA

- Nalanda was a Buddhist **monastery** in the kingdom of Magadha in India.
- People came to the monastery to get an education.
- It was built around 427 BCE.

EVENTS DURING ANCIENT INDIA

CA. 7000 BCE The Harappan civilization starts to grow.

CA. 1500 BCE The Vedic people enter the Indus River valley.

600 BCE The 16 Mahajanapadas come to power in northeast India.

CA. 550 BCE The Persian Empire takes over northwest India.

500–400 BCE Buddhism spreads throughout India.

327 BCE Alexander the Great conquers parts of India.

321 BCE The Mauryan Empire is formed.

CA. 240 CE The Gupta Empire is formed.

CA. 550 CE The Gupta Empire ends.

GLOSSARY

archaeologist: Someone who studies the tools and other objects left behind by ancient people.

conquer: To take by force.

culture: The beliefs and ways of life of a group of people.

decline: To become worse in condition or quality.

enlightened: Having an open mind and showing a good understanding of how people should be treated.

expert: Someone with a special skill or knowledge.

influence: To have an effect on.

monastery: A community of religious people who have chosen to separate themselves from the world to focus on their religion.

physical: Relating to the body of a person instead of the mind; existing in a form that can be seen and touched.

standardize: To make the same.

strict: Demanding that people obey rules or behave in a certain way.

subcontinent: A large area of land that is a part of one of Earth's seven major landmasses.

symbol: A picture, shape, or object that stands for something else.

FIND OUT MORE

BOOKS

Cooke, Tim. *The Indus Valley Civilisation*. London, UK: Franklin Watts, 2019.

Green, Sara. *Ancient India*. Minneapolis, MN: Bellwether Media, 2020.

Johnson, Anne. *Exploring Ancient India*. Mankato, MN: 12 Story Library, 2018.

WEBSITES

Ancient India for Kids
india.mrdonn.org
Students can read about ancient India and play games to test their knowledge.

The British Museum: Ancient India
www.ancientindia.co.uk
Pictures, stories, and activities make ancient India come alive.

NeoK12: History of India
https://www.neok12.com/History-of-India.htm
Watch videos that explain India's history from prehistoric to modern times.

INDEX